CAN I *Mix* YOU A
DRINK?

COCKTAILS FROM **50** MY LIFE & CAREER

T-PAIN
with MAXWELL BRITTEN

T-PAIN
with MAXWELL BRITTEN

CAN I *Mix* YOU A
DRINK?

COCKTAILS FROM **50** MY LIFE & CAREER

T-PAIN
with MAXWELL BRITTEN

CAN I *Mix* YOU A
DRINK?

COCKTAILS FROM **50** MY LIFE & CAREER

T-PAIN
with MAXWELL BRITTEN

COCKTAILS FROM **50** MY LIFE & CAREER

CAN I *Mix* YOU A
DRIN

CAN I *Mix* YOU A
DRINK?

COCKTAILS FROM **50** MY LIFE & CAREER

T-PAIN
with MAXWELL BRITTEN

T-PAIN
with MAXWELL BRITTEN

CAN I *Mix* YOU A
DRINK?

COCKTAILS FROM **50** MY LIFE & CAREER **50**

CAN I *Mix* YOU A DRINK?

50
COCKTAILS FROM MY LIFE & CAREER

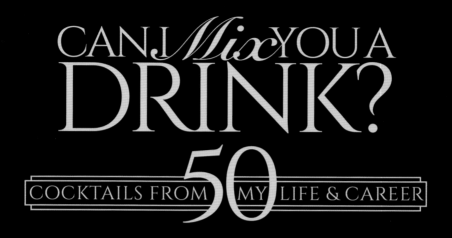

T-PAIN
with MAXWELL BRITTEN

KINGSTON IMPERIAL, NEW YORK, NY

TABLE
CONTE

DEDICATION

In loving memory of my brother Rasheed Constantine Najm. You're usually

supposed to pour one out, but now the world will pour one up for you.

Good God almighty, if anyone would've told me that at the tender lovin' age of thirty-six I'd be writing my own damn book with recipes of drinks named after my own multi–platinum, Grammy Award–winning songs, I would've told them: *You're goddamn right!*

I'm just fuckin' with ya. But I've gotta admit, ever since I picked up a pen in one hand to write my first song, I had a beer in the other. Alcohol and music always went hand in hand for me. I had to break the seal, though.

So, the first time I ever got drunk, I was fifteen years old. See, they don't sell a 40 ounce over in Florida like they do everywhere else. We have a 32 ounce, which apparently was enough to knock *me* on my ass. My friend was older, so he's the one who I can blame for starting my drunken shenanigans, and I guess he's the reason for this book, really. He bought me a 32 ounce and told me, "You'll know you're drunk when your legs get numb." A few gulps in and my limbs fell off. Somehow I put them back on, headed home to my dad's house, and threw up everywhere. I woke up on my bathroom floor. Vomit was all over the place—in the tub, on the shower, in the sink, on the floor, and even in the toilet where it belonged. It smelled like vomit and beer, which is a scent that will *never* have its own candle. My dumb ass was fifteen, so I didn't think about cleaning it up. I just sat there lookin' at it. My dad walked in, looked at me, looked at the vomit, and said, "Well, you drink now, I guess. Clean that shit up."

That was not the last time that I ever drank; in fact, it gave me the courage to just keep going. My legs were still on and I didn't die, so I was unstoppable!

I would sit in the backyard with my friend, listening to some R&B songs with a beer in my hand, catching a buzz and writing my own jams to the structure of hits by other singers. We would sit there for fucking hours and hours and just drink beer and listen to songs and say, "Well, listen, he puts hooks together like this . . . But let's see how the beat came up there . . . Like he did this . . ." And we would just study and study and study and study. That's how I learned how to write a hit song—drunk of my ass. I think so many of my songs are about alcohol because of how I got started writing them.

By the way, I'm T-Pain, the captain of the Nappy Boy ship, Mr. Teddy Penderazdoun, Teddy Verseti, and everybody's favorite rappa turnt sanga. Chances are you've spent at least three nights in your life making a bad decision while you were drunk and my music was the soundtrack. For that, I am proud. Listen, there is way too much bullshit going on in the world to not take a few minutes to enjoy ourselves. It's our right and if that means taking a couple of sips of something toxic but not deadly to feel good, then hell, go on then.

For years, I was just all about beer. I didn't graduate to the top shelf at the bar until 2003, when I was with my group Nappy Headz. We finally got to touring, hitting a couple of dates and getting more popular. I remember we had a stop in Alabama and we went to this club, and they asked us what we wanted to drink. It was free! We didn't know a damn thing about expensive liquor, so they gave us Moët & Chandon's Nectar Impérial. I couldn't stop drinkin' it. Once you get the taste of that sweet honey, then beer starts to taste like fifteen-year-old me's vomit on the bathroom floor.

The more popular I became, the more the liquor flowed. Then I started learning about more and more drink options. I remember I was in Russia this one time before I was a vodka drinker, and they offered me vodka. I said, "I don't drink that," and they said to me, "The hell you don't!" You don't turn down vodka from Russians, apparently. How should I know Russian customs? So that's how I started drinking vodka.

I wouldn't be the drinker that I am if I wasn't T-Pain, that's for sure. It's the fact that I get free drinks all the time. I wrote a song called "Buy U a Drank?" knowing damn well the drink I was giving the girl was probably free. Either that or she was going to take my lukewarm cup of Hennessy while I went and got a fresh one. But don't tell *her* that. It was basically like the whole world was enabling me everywhere I went. They just gave me free drinks, and you know, what am I gonna do? Sit at the table not drinking it? I'm polite.

Truth is, I didn't plan on reaching this level. I'm from Tallahassee, Florida, and even though there's a lot of people there, it's got such a small-town mentality. Part of me held on to that mindset, where I couldn't even fathom becoming famous. Even just moving to Atlanta was a big challenge for me, because there were already enough people there singing and rapping and shit. Coming into the industry and thinking that you're gonna be the hottest is just fucking insane. It doesn't happen. It's like playing football in middle school and being like, "I'm for sure going to the NFL." But somehow it happened for me, and I'm happy to be here.

So let me tell you why I put together *Can I Mix You a Drink?* . . .

There came a time when I would go to the bar at any club, and the bartender would take too damn long to fix me my drink. I don't know what he or she was doing behind that bar, but it would take forever, and I was trying to get a little buzz. Eventually, I would just say, "Hey, man! Just pour me a glass of brown liquor, OK? Let's save some time here." Then, once I started spending more time at home, I realized I didn't want to just pour a glass and sit there. I wanted the good stuff, the fun stuff. I married a mixologist, for crying out loud. I deserved better for my drinks at home. So what did I do? I created my own bible of traditional drinks with a T-Pain twist, plus some concoctions you've never even heard of before. This is for everyone who isn't at the bar as much these days. For the people who want to mix some good shit up at home and who want it to look good, like they're the greatest expert mixologist to ever hold a glass, fill it with ice, mix it, and pour it. I titled all of these drinks after my songs, because again, my music and my liquor go hand in hand.

So get your ingredients ready, and let's make some bad decisions in the comfort of our own homes. And if you act a little too stupid, just blame it on the alcohol.

– T-Pain

DRANKS

OH, I'M FANCY

When this whole pandemic mess started, I knew I needed a really meaningful glass to drink out of because I'd be spending most of my nights sippin' somethin' either at home or in my studio. So I went to this boutique in, like, the weird part of Atlanta. You know, the type of store that sells random fucking books, pillows made out of cat hair, and phone cases with cartoon dicks on them. Then I spotted this glass with "Fancy" written on it in gold, and hell, I needed something fancy in my life. I can never have enough fancy. Fancy me up, I say. So I bought the glass, and it hasn't left my side. It's a win-win if you ask me, because now I can drink all these drinks in it.

Shawty

SHAWTY

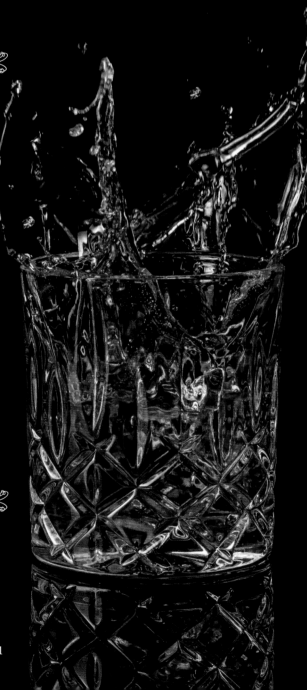

Style: Stirred

Base: Bourbon

Ingredients:
2 ounces Fistful of Bourbon
5 ounces White Crème de Cacao
3 dashes orange bitters
2 dashes aromatic bitters

Glass: Double rocks

Ice: Large cube for serving, cubed ice for stirring

Garnish: Lemon twist, orange twist

Tools: mixing glass, julep strainer, mixing Spoon,
Ounce Jigger

Methodology:
Add all ingredients into mixing glass, add as
much ice as possible and stir for 30 seconds.
Strain into chilled glass. Carefully twist the citrus
peels one at a time over glass to express oils,
discard and serve.

7 Up

1 UP

Style: Shaken

Base: Vodka

Ingredients:
1½ ounces Smirnoff Iced Cake Vodka
4 drops Bitter End Thai bitters
¾ ounce fresh lime juice
¾ ounce fresh pineapple
Topped with club soda

Glass: Highball

Ice: Crushed ice

Garnish: Dehydrated pineapple, lime wedge,
fresh mint

Tools: Boston shaker, Hawthorne strainer, fine
strainer, ounce jigger, paring knife, mixing spoon

Methodology:
Combine all ingredients in Boston shaker
omitting club soda: add ice, hard shake, double
strain, top with club soda, stir and garnish.

Special Ingredients:
Dehydrated Pineapple
Dehydrated fruit can be store bought or special
ordered.

5 O'Clock

5 O'CLOCK

Style: Built in Glass

Base: Bourbon

Ingredients:
1 ounce Fistful of Bourbon
½ ounce Goldschläger liqueur
2 scoops of Häagen-Dazs or Ben & Jerry's
vanilla ice cream
Topped with stout beer

Glass: Stemmed beer glass

Ice: No ice

Garnish: Whipped cream, edible gold flakes

Tools: Ounce jigger, ice cream scoop

Methodology:
Freeze Glass before serving, set aside. Use two
full scoops quality vanilla ice cream. Pour over
bourbon, Goldschläger and top with the beer
leaving at least ½ inch before reaching the top
of the glass. Top w/ lightly whipped cream and
gold flakes.

THE BEST DRINKING GAME

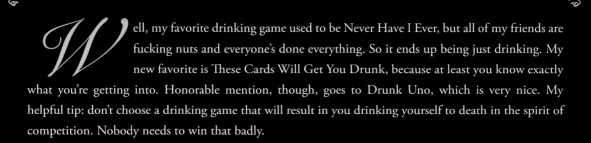

*W*ell, my favorite drinking game used to be Never Have I Ever, but all of my friends are fucking nuts and everyone's done everything. So it ends up being just drinking. My new favorite is These Cards Will Get You Drunk, because at least you know exactly what you're getting into. Honorable mention, though, goes to Drunk Uno, which is very nice. My helpful tip: don't choose a drinking game that will result in you drinking yourself to death in the spirit of competition. Nobody needs to win that badly.

Bang Bang
Low Low

18

BANG BANG POW POW

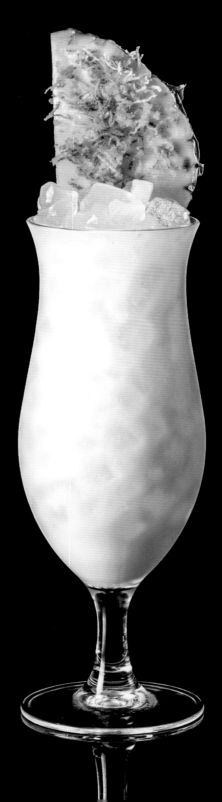

Style: Built in glass and swizzled

Base: Tequila

Ingredients:
2 ounces Jalapeño-Infused Espolon Blanco Tequila
1 ounce evaporated milk
1 ounce fresh pineapple juice
½ ounce fresh lime juice
½ ounce simple syrup

Glass: Hurricane glass

Ice: Crushed

Garnish: Pineapple slice, lime zest, orange zest

Tools: Ounce jigger, swizzle stick, paring knife, Microplane

Methodology:
Build all ingredients into glass. Fill with crushed ice and swizzle. Add more crushed ice to top up the glass if needed and garnish.

Special Ingredients:
Jalapeño-Infused Tequila
750 milliliters bottle of Espolon Blanco Tequila
3–4 sliced green jalapeños without seeds

Combine all ingredients in a quart container with a lid. Give it a nice shake and let sit for 30 minutes. Routinely taste to determine level of heat. It should have a good kick but not so strong that you can't knock it back. Peppers vary in heat scale, so you will need to keep checking.

Simple Syrup
1½ cups room-temperature water
1½ cups granulated sugar

Combine Equal Parts Water to Sugar over low heat. Stir until sugar and water have fully integrated, add orange bitters and stir. Bring to room temperature then refrigerate for two hours.

Tipsy

TIPSY

Style: Shaken

Base: Tequila

Ingredients:
1 ounce Hiatus Tequila Blanco
½ ounce spicy honey syrup
1 ounce fresh pineapple juice
½ ounce fresh lemon juice
Topped with Dos Equis beer

Glass: Highball

Ice: Cubed

Garnish: Smoked Chipotle Salt Rimmer, pineapple spear

Tools: Ounce jigger, mixing spoon, paring knife

Methodology:
Prepare a frozen glass, rim, add ice, build all ingredients into glass omitting the beer. Once everything has been added, give a brief stir, top beer, stir again until beer has fully been topped up and garnish.

Special Ingredients:
Spicy Honey Syrup
Honey Syrup
1 cup premium honey
1 cup water
1 small sliced jalapeño, seeds removed

Combine Equal Parts Water to Honey over low heat. Stir until honey and water have fully integrated. Add sliced jalapeño and simmer for 15 minutes. Bring to room temperature then refrigerate for 1 hour with jalapeño and strain.

Smoked Salt/Chipotle Rimmer
1 tablespoon smoked salt
1 tablespoon smoked paprika
½ tablespoon Tajín seasoning

Combine 1 tablespoon smoked salt, 1 tablespoon smoked paprika, ½ tablespoon tajin. Use mortar and pestle for uniform coarse texture.

MY SOUNDTRACK TO GETTING FUCKED UP

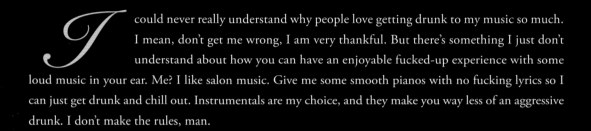

I could never really understand why people love getting drunk to my music so much. I mean, don't get me wrong, I am very thankful. But there's something I just don't understand about how you can have an enjoyable fucked-up experience with some loud music in your ear. Me? I like salon music. Give me some smooth pianos with no fucking lyrics so I can just get drunk and chill out. Instrumentals are my choice, and they make you way less of an aggressive drunk. I don't make the rules, man.

Calm The Fuck Down

CALM THE FUCK DOWN

Style: Shaken

Base: Pimm's

Ingredients:
2 ounces Pimm's No. 1 Cup liqueur
2 ounces coconut water
4 drops CBD oil
1 tablespoon blueberry jam or preserves
1 Small bunch wild arugula
Topped with ginger beer

Glass: Highball

Ice: Cubed

Garnish: Fresh mint, candied ginger, skewered blueberries, coconut flakes

Tools: Ounce jigger, Boston shaker, Hawthorne strainer, fine strainer

Methodology:
Without muddling add all ingredients together in Boston shaker omitting ginger beer and shake hard with ice then double strain into glass, top w/ ginger beer. Carefully add ice and top up only if necessary, then stir, garnish.

Special Ingredients:
Blueberry Jam
Blueberry jam or preserves can be store bought. I recommend Bonne Maman Wild Blueberry Preserves.

Candied Ginger
Candied ginger can be store bought or special ordered.

CHOPPED N
SKREWED

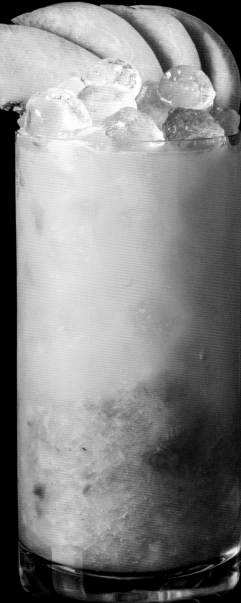

Style: Built in glass

Base: Vodka

Ingredients:
2 ounces Grey Goose Vodka
¾ ounce Giffard Crème de Pêche de Vigne liqueur
3 ounces fresh orange juice
4 dashes orange-flower water
1 pinch sea salt
2–3 slices fresh peach

Glass: Collins

Ice: Crushed

Garnish: Fanned peaches

Tools: Muddler, ounce jigger, Boston shaker,
Hawthorne strainer, fine strainer, paring knife

Methodology:
Add fresh peach slices to glass, muddle and set aside.
Build all ingredients in Boston Shaker. Shake hard
with ice, double strain into glass over ice, garnish.

Church

CHURCH

Style: Shaken

Base: Beaujolais

Ingredients:
2 ounces Beaujolais
2 dashes Angostura bitters
½ ounce crème de fraise
½ ounce Campari
½ ounce 1:1 simple syrup
½ ounce tart cherry juice
2 sliced oranges
2 whole strawberries
2 cucumber slices

Glass: Wine or rocks glass

Ice: Cubed

Garnish: Strawberry, cucumber ribbon,
blood orange wheel

Tools: Paring knife, Y peeler, mixing spoon, muddler,
Boston shaker, Hawthorne strainer, fine strainer

Methodology:
Muddle oranges, strawberries, and cucumbers in
Boston shaker. Add wine, cherry juice, crème de
fraise, Campari, bitters, and simple syrup. Add ice,
shake, and double strain into glass over ice. Add more
ice if needed, garnish, and serve.

Special Ingredients:
Simple Syrup
1½ cups room-temperature water
1½ cups granulated sugar

Combine equal parts water to sugar in a pan over
low heat. Stir until sugar and water have fully
integrated, add orange bitters and stir. Bring to room
temperature then refrigerate for two hours.

T-PAIN'S FIRST GOLDEN RULE OF DRINKING LIKE A PRO

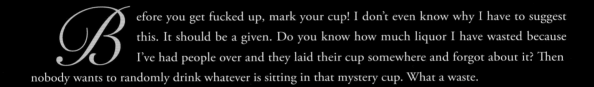

Before you get fucked up, mark your cup! I don't even know why I have to suggest this. It should be a given. Do you know how much liquor I have wasted because I've had people over and they laid their cup somewhere and forgot about it? Then nobody wants to randomly drink whatever is sitting in that mystery cup. What a waste.

Cartel

CARTEL

Style: Shaken

Base: Mezcal

Ingredients:
¾ ounce Casamigos Joven Mezcal
¾ ounce Maraschino liqueur
¾ ounce Green Chartreuse
¾ ounce fresh lime juice

Glass: Coupe

Ice: Cubed for shaking only

Garnish: Smoked salt, powdered chipotle rim

Tools: Ounce jigger, Boston shaker, Hawthorne strainer, fine strainer

Methodology:
Rim serving glass with garnish and set aside.
Combine all ingredients in Boston shaker, add ice,
shake hard, double strain into glass, and serve.

Speciality Ingredients:
Smoked Salt/Chipotle Rimmer
1 tablespoon smoked salt
1 tablespoon smoked paprika
½ tablespoon Tajín seasoning

Combine all ingredients in a mortar and grind up
with pestle for uniform coarse texture.

Cyclone

CYCLONE

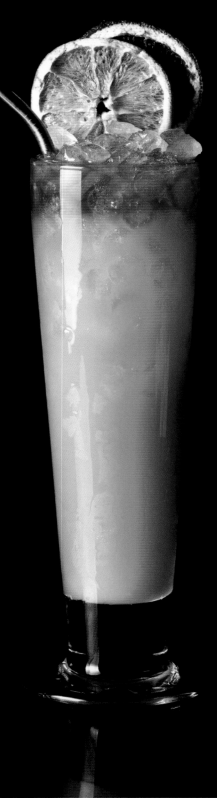

Style: Built in glass and swizzled

Base: Rum

Ingredients:
2 ounces Ron del Barrilito 3 Star rum
½ ounce Blue Curaçao
½ ounce Campari
1 ounce fresh lemon juice
1 ounce coconut syrup

Glass: Pilsner

Ice: Crushed

Garnish: Dehydrated orange wheels, straw

Tools: Ounce jigger, swizzle stick

Methodology:
Build all ingredients except the Campari in glass. Fill with crushed ice and swizzle. Add more crushed ice to top up the glass. Pour Campari over the top, garnish, and serve.

Special Ingredients:
Dehydrated Orange Wheels
Dehydrated fruit can be store bought or special ordered.

Coconut Syrup
15 ounces Coconut milk
15 ounces Coconut cream

Combine equal parts coconut milk to coconut cream in a pan over low heat for 15 minutes. Let cool to room temperature, then refrigerate for 2 hours. For longer shelf life, always refrigerate. Be sure to give the syrup a shake or stir before using.

Darkskin Debarge

DARKSKIN DEBARGE

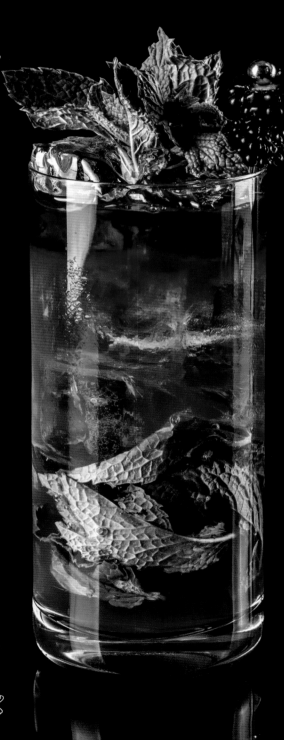

Style: Shaken

Base: Rum

Ingredients:
1½ ounces Hamilton Jamaican Pot Still Black rum
¾ ounce fresh lime juice
½ ounce simple syrup
½ ounce Cruzan Blackstrap rum float
1 small bunch loose mint
Topped with ginger beer

Glass: Highball

Ice: Cubed

Garnish: Fresh mint, Blackstrap rum float, halved blackberries

Tools: Boston shaker, Hawthorne strainer, fine strainer, ounce jigger, paring knife, mixing spoon, muddler

Methodology:
Muddle mint in serving glass and set aside. Combine rum, simple syrup, fresh lime juice, and ice in Boston shaker, shake hard, and strain into glass. Add ice, top with ginger beer, then stir. Float the Blackstrap rum at the top, garnish, and serve.

Specialty Ingredient:
Simple Syrup
1½ cups room-temperature water
1½ cups granulated sugar

Combine equal parts water to sugar in a pan over low heat. Stir until sugar has dissolved, add orange bitters and stir. Let cool to room temperature, then refrigerate for 2 hours before using. For longer shelf life, always keep refrigerated.

F.B.G.M.

F.B.G.M.

Style: Built in Glass

Base: Gin

Ingredients:
2 ounces Fennel-Infused Gin
2 dashes celery bitters
Topped with tonic water

Glass: Collins

Ice: Cubed

Garnish: Pink peppercorns, fresh mint, grapefruit slice, lemon and grapefruit twists

Tools: Ounce jigger, mixing spoon, paring knife or peeler

Methodology:
Build gin and bitters in glass. Top with tonic water and carefully add ice. Stir and top again if needed. Garnish with all items saving the lemon and grapefruit twist to the end. Carefully twist the citrus peels one at a time over glass to express oils, discard peels, add the rest of garnishes and serve.

Special Ingredients:
Fennel-Infused Gin
6 bulbs of fresh fennel
750 milliliters dry gin

Finely chop fennel bulbs and put in 1-gallon zip-lock plastic bag. Add gin, seal tightly, and refrigerate with bag sitting upright for 24 hours. Strain out fennel and re-bottle gin for use.

Celery Bitters
Celery bitters can be store bought.
I recommend The Bitter Truth bitters.

Best Love Song

BEST
LOVE SONG

Style: Shaken

Base: Gin

Ingredients:
1 ounce Dorothy Parker gin
1½ ounces Rockey's liqueur
5 cucumber slices
Topped with sparkling rosé moscato

Glass: Wine glass

Ice: Cubed

Garnish: Cucumber wheels

Tools: Ounce jigger, Boston shaker, muddler,
Hawthorne strainer, fine strainer, paring knife,
mixing spoon

Methodology:
Combine gin and Rockey's in Boston shaker and
muddle with approximately 5 cucumber slices.
Shake with 1 ice cube and double strain into
glass. Add ice, top with sparkling rosé moscato,
garnish, and serve.

FLIGHT SCHOOL

Style: Built in glass

Base: Whiskey

Ingredients:
2 ounces Jack Daniel's Tennessee Honey whiskey ½ cup hot English breakfast tea

Glass: Teacup on saucer

Ice: No ice

Garnish: Sugar cubes, lemon twist, spoon, biscuit crackers, hot nuts

Tools: Ounce jigger, tea set, paring knife or peeler

Methodology:
Pour Tennessee Honey into teacup, then pour over freshly brewed hot black tea (English breakfast). Tea should be brewed on its own and cocktail should not be served with any remnants of the tea brew or tea bags. After tea has been poured over it is recommended to add a twist of lemon over the drink and add a sugar cube to be stirred in by your guest.

Fly Away

FLY AWAY

Style: Built in Glass

Base: Rum

Ingredients:
¾ ounce Wray & Nephew rum
½ ounce Butterscotch schnapps
½ ounce fresh lemon juice
4 drops orange-flower water
Topped with Cherry Coke

Glass: Highball

Ice: Cubed

Garnish: Candied orange, lime wheel, lemon twist

Tools: Ounce jigger, mixing spoon, paring knife

Methodology:
Build all ingredients except the Cherry Coke in glass.
Add ice, top with Cherry Coke, stir and top again if
needed, then garnish and serve.

Specialty Ingredient:
Candied Orange
Candied fruit can be store bought or special ordered.

T-PAIN'S SECOND GOLDEN RULE OF DRINKING LIKE A PRO

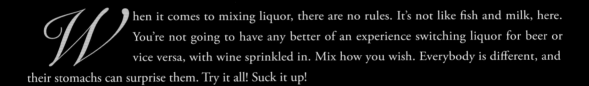

When it comes to mixing liquor, there are no rules. It's not like fish and milk, here. You're not going to have any better of an experience switching liquor for beer or vice versa, with wine sprinkled in. Mix how you wish. Everybody is different, and their stomachs can surprise them. Try it all! Suck it up!

FREEZE

Style: Blended

Base: Tequila

Ingredients:
6 ounces Casamigos Reposado tequila
3¾ ounces Combier triple sec
3¾ ounces fresh lime juice
3¾ ounces pink guava purée
2 teaspoons sea salt

Glass: Coupe

Ice: Cubed or crushed for blending

Garnish: Half salt rim with halved guava

Tools: Blender, measuring cup for ice, paring knife

Methodology:
Combine all ingredients in a blender. Add 2 heavy
cups of ice and pulse until ice has been dissolved.
Garnish one side of glass rims with salt and the other
side with halved guava, then pour. Serves four.

Specialty Ingredients:
Guava Purée
Guava purée can be store bought or special ordered.
I recommend The Perfect Purée.

Goat Talk

GOAT TALK

Style: Shaken

Base: Cognac

Ingredients:
1 ounce D'Ussé cognac
½ ounce fresh blood-orange juice
¼ ounce fresh lemon juice
½ ounce simple syrup
Topped with Armand de Brignac "Ace of Spades"
Champagne

Glass: Flute

Ice: Cubed for shaking only

Garnish: Large lemon twist

Tools: Ounce jigger, Boston shaker, Hawthorne
strainer, fine strainer, paring knife or peeler

Methodology:
Combine all ingredients except the champagne in
Boston shaker. Add ice, give it a hard shake, double
strain into glass, and top up with Ace of Spades,
then garnish and serve.

Special Ingredients
Simple Syrup
1½ cups room-temperature water
1½ cups granulated sugar

Combine equal parts water to sugar in a pan over low
heat. Stir until sugar and water have fully integrated, add
orange bitters and stir. Let cool to room temperature,
then refrigerate for 2 hours before using. For longer shelf
life, always keep refrigerated.

T-PAIN'S THIRD GOLDEN RULE OF DRINKING LIKE A PRO

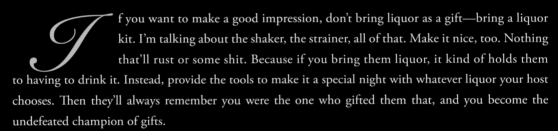

*I*f you want to make a good impression, don't bring liquor as a gift—bring a liquor kit. I'm talking about the shaker, the strainer, all of that. Make it nice, too. Nothing that'll rust or some shit. Because if you bring them liquor, it kind of holds them to having to drink it. Instead, provide the tools to make it a special night with whatever liquor your host chooses. Then they'll always remember you were the one who gifted them that, and you become the undefeated champion of gifts.

Got Money

GOT MONEY

Style: Shaken

Base: Gin

Ingredients:
1½ ounces Dorothy Parker gin
½ ounce Lillet
¼ ounce white crème de cacao
½ ounce fresh lemon juice
1 teaspoon matcha powder
1 egg white

Glass: Coupe

Ice: Cubed ice for shaking only

Garnish: Lemon twist, powdered matcha

Tools: Ounce jigger, Boston shaker, Hawthorne strainer, fine strainer, paring knife or peeler

Methodology:
Combine all ingredients in Boston shaker, adding egg white last. Dry shake very hard for 15 to 20 seconds. Add ice and hard shake for 20 seconds. Double strain into glass. Carefully twist the citrus peel over glass to express oils, and discard peel. Add matcha powder garnish, and serve.

Special Ingredients:
Matcha Powder
Matcha powder can be store bought.
I recommend Jade Leaf Culinary Matcha.

Booty Werk

BOOTY WERK

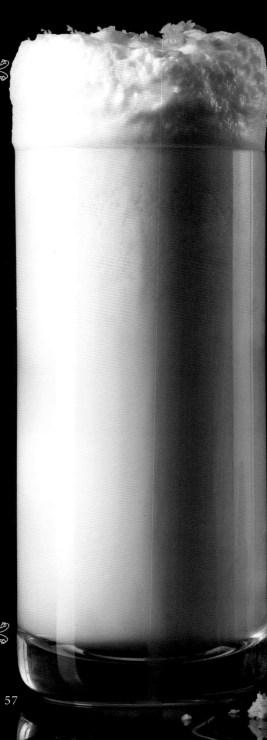

Style: Shaken

Base: Vodka

Ingredients:
1½ ounces Cîroc Summer Citrus
½ ounce fresh lime juice
½ ounce fresh lemon juice
2 dashes orange bitters
1 ounce heavy cream
3 drops orange-flower water
Topped with Red Bull

Glass: Highball

Ice: Cubed for shaking only

Garnish: Shaved orange zest, lemon twist

Tools: Ounce jigger, Boston shaker, Hawthorne strainer, fine strainer, paring knife or peeler, microplane

Methodology:
Prepare a frozen glass and set aside. Combine all ingredients except the Red Bull in Boston shaker in the following order: Cîroc, orange-flower water, orange bitters, heavy cream, lemon juice, and lime juice. Dry shake for 15 seconds, then add ice and hard shake for 25 seconds. Double strain into frozen glass and carefully top with Red Bull. Carefully twist the citrus peel over glass to express oils, and discard peel. Garnish and serve.

All I Do Is Win

IS WIN

Style: Shaken

Base: Bourbon

Ingredients:
1½ ounces Fistful of Bourbon
½ ounce simple syrup
2 orange slices
3 lemon slices
1 small bunch loose mint
2 dashes Angostura bitters
Topped with club soda

Glass: Highball

Ice: Cubed

Garnish: Fresh mint, lemon wheel

Tools: Ounce jigger, Boston shaker, muddler, Hawthorne strainer, fine strainer, paring knife, mixing spoon

Methodology:
Combine bourbon, orange and lemon slices, mint, bitters, and simple syrup in Boston shaker and muddle. Add ice, shake hard, and double strain into glass. Top with club soda, garnish, and serve.

Special Ingredients:
Simple Syrup
1½ cups room-temperature water
1½ cups granulated sugar

Combine equal parts water to sugar in a pan over low heat. Stir until sugar has dissolved. Let cool to room temperature, then refrigerate for 2 hours before using. For longer shelf life, always keep refrigerated.

I'm High

I'M HIGH

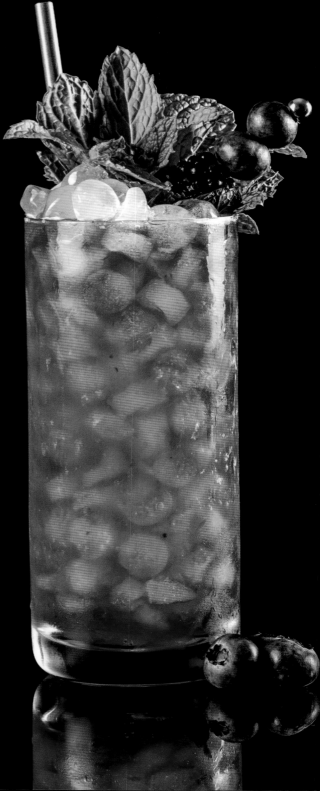

Style: Shaken

Base: Sloe Gin

Ingredients:
2 ounces Plymouth Sloe Gin
½ ounce crème de cassis
1 ounce fresh lemon juice
½ ounce simple syrup
6 drops CBD oil
1 tablespoon blueberry jam or preserves

Glass: Highball

Ice: Crushed

Garnish: Skewered fresh blueberries and blackberries, fresh mint, straw

Tools: Ounce jigger, Boston shaker, paring knife, mixing spoon

Methodology:
Combine all ingredients in Boston shaker, including blueberry jam. Add crushed ice, shake briefly, and dump all contents of the shaker into the serving glass. Top up with more crushed ice, garnish, and serve.

Special Ingredients:
Blueberry Jam
Blueberry jam or preserves can be store bought. I recommend Bonne Maman Wild Blueberry Preserves.

Simple Syrup
1½ cups room-temperature water
1½ cups granulated sugar

Combine equal parts water to sugar in a pan over low heat. Stir until sugar and water have fully integrated, add orange bitters and stir. Let cool to room temperature, then refrigerate for 2 hours before using. For longer shelf life, always keep refrigerated.

THE FIVE MOST EXPENSIVE LIQUOR BRANDS
I'VE EVER PURCHASED WHILE SOBER

1. Hennessy Richard—I think I bought this one for an anniversary or something. I got it at the airport at one of those duty-free joints. It was like $7,000. Very cool.

2. Louis XIII Cognac—Obviously.

3. Hennessy Paradis—This one was like $900 a shot.

4. Grey Goose Magnum—It takes like two people to pour it. It's a very stupidly and famously large bottle, purely for showing off.

5. Macallan 25—Not quite Macallan 52, but still good.

I'm On A Boat

I'M ON A BOAT

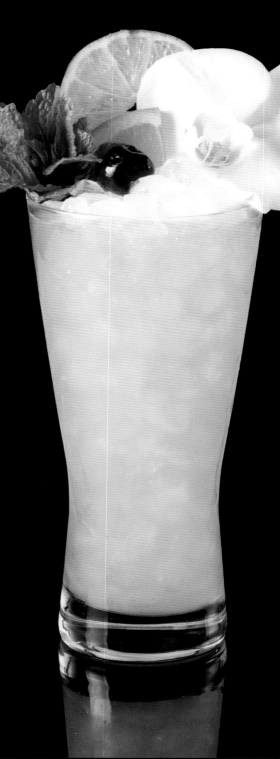

Style: Built in glass and swizzled

Base: Cachaça

Ingredients:
2 ounces Avuá Prata cachaça
1½ ounces fresh pineapple juice
1 ounce fresh orange juice
1 ounce coconut syrup

Glass: Pilsner

Ice: Crushed

Garnish: Lime wheel, edible orchid, fresh mint, orange slice, aged cocktail cherry

Tools: Ounce jigger, swizzle stick

Methodology:
Build all ingredients in glass. Fill with crushed ice and swizzle. Add more crushed ice to top up the glass, then garnish and serve.

Special Ingredients:
Coconut Syrup
15 ounces coconut milk
15 ounces coconut cream

Combine equal parts coconut milk to coconut syrup in a pan over low heat for 15 minutes. Let cool to room temperature, then refrigerate for 2 hours. For longer shelf life, always refrigerate. Be sure to give the syrup a shake or stir before using.

I'm So Hood

I'M SO HOOD

Style: Shaken

Base: Cognac

Ingredients:
1 ounce D'Ussé Cognac
½ ounce fresh lemon juice
½ ounce Olde English Reduction
Topped with Moët champagne

Glass: Large cocktail glass or goblet

Ice: Cubed for shaking only

Garnish: Lemon twist, small paper bag

Tools: Ounce jigger, Boston shaker, Hawthorne
strainer, fine strainer, paring knife or peeler

Methodology:
Combine all ingredients except the champagne in
Boston Shaker. Add ice and give a hard shake, then
double strain into glass. Top with champagne,
garnish, and serve.

Special Ingredients:
Old English Reduction
40 ounces Olde English malt liquor
5 cups granulated sugar
4 cinnamon sticks
4 anise pods
6 cardamom pods

In a large saucepan, add Olde English and spices.
Heat to a simmer on medium, 10 minutes. Once
liquid is indicated as heated, reduce heat to low
and slowly stir in sugar. Once all sugar has been
fully dissolved, bring heat back up to a simmer.
Periodically stir for 30 minutes. Remove from heat
and allow to cool to room temperature. Let chill
in the fridge in an uncovered nonmetal container.
Strain out spices before using in recipe and keep
refrigerated covered for long term shelf life.

THE BEST
BOTTOM SHELF LIQUOR
TO DRINK WHEN YOU'RE BROKE OR JUST TRYING TO BE POLITE AROUND BROKE PEOPLE

1. Meukow Cognac

2. E&J Brandy

3. Zima

I'm Sprung

I'M SPRUNG

Style: Built in glass

Base: Wine

Ingredients:
3 ounces dry Riesling
1 ounce Giffard Crème de Pêche de Vigne liqueur
½ ounce fresh lemon juice
4 drops orange-flower water
Topped with LaCroix mango sparkling water

Glass: Wine glass

Ice: Cubed

Garnish: Fresh mint, orange wheel, strawberry slices, straw

Tools: Ounce jigger, mixing spoon, paring knife

Methodology:
Build all ingredients except the LaCroix in glass. Top with a little sparkling water, then carefully top with ice. Stir and top again, garnish, and serve.

Hey Baby
(Drop It To The Floor)

HEY BABY
(DROP IT TO THE FLOOR)

Style: Built in glass

Base: Brandy

Ingredients:
1½ ounces D'Ussé Cognac
½ ounce Maraschino liqueur
½ ounce Heering cherry liqueur
½ ounce Bénédictine liqueur
1 ounce fresh lime juice
½ ounce fresh pineapple juice
2 dashes aromatic bitters

Glass: Hurricane glass

Ice: Crushed

Garnish: Pineapple leaves, lime wheel, aged cocktail cherry, straw

Tools: Ounce jigger, swizzle stick, paring knife

Methodology:
Build all ingredients in glass. Add crushed ice, swizzle for 10 seconds, top with more crushed ice, garnish, and serve.

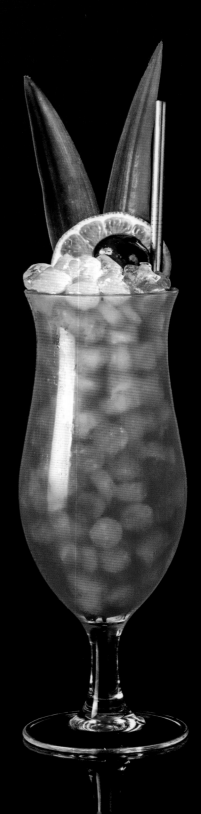

KISS KISS

Style: Shaken

Base: Apple Brandy

Ingredients:
1½ ounces White Applejack
1 ounce Rockey's liqueur
¼ ounce Vieux Pontarlier Verte Absinthe
¾ ounce fresh lime juice
¼ ounce honey syrup

Glass: Coupe

Ice: Cubed for shaking only

Garnish: Lime twist

Tools: Ounce jigger, Boston shaker, Hawthorne
strainer, fine strainer, paring knife or Y peeler

Methodology:
Combine all ingredients in Boston shaker, add ice,
shake hard, double strain into glass, garnish, and serve.

Special Ingredients:
Honey Syrup
1 cup premium honey
1 cup water

Combine equal parts water to honey in a pan over
low heat. Stir until honey and water have fully
integrated. Let cool to room temperature, then
refrigerate for 2 hours before use. Shake, stir or agitate
at all times of use. For longer shelf life always keep
refrigerated.

STRIP CLUB ETIQUETTE

*Y*ou don't just show up to a strip club with some ones balled up in your pocket, ready to rock. Who raised you if you think that's a good idea? Well, this is your father speaking: it's not! When I hit the strip club, it's strategic. I have a trick to tip the dancers, which is what I like to call "the flying sausage." Now that's where you roll up some ones and you launch them at the dancer and then they explode into a beautiful bouquet of bills. You have to cap it at fourteen dollars, though, or else it's like you're throwing a rock at her. I mean, you also don't have to use ones, but we are still in a recession (I think).

Now, here's the real cheat code: the liquor choice. Don't try and be cute with the champagne or even grab your go-to drink that you'd order at another club. My choice? Wine. I have reasons for this. For one, it's classier, and we are watching the art of exotic dance, for crying out loud. Two, you're not too fucked up to start randomly throwing your money on the ground, which brings me to three, which is that I can still make it home, and if there's sex when I get back home, then I can actually remember what happened. There's a way less chance of "whiskey dick." Anything else feels like a bad hangover waiting to happen, leaving me broke and with a headache. No thanks.

All The Above

ALL THE ABOVE

Style: Shaken

Base: Mezcal

Ingredients:
2 ounces Casamigos Joven Mezcal
¾ ounce Cointreau liqueur
¼ ounce Campari liqueur
½ ounce fresh lime juice
½ ounce raspberry syrup

Glass: Coupe

Ice: Cubed for shaking only

Garnish: Skewered raspberries

Tools: Ounce jigger, Boston shaker,
Hawthorne strainer, fine strainer

Methodology:
Combine all ingredients in Boston shaker. Shake hard
with ice, double strain into glass, garnish, and serve.

Special Ingredients:
Raspberry Syrup
1 quart 1:1 simple syrup (room temperature)
1 pint raspberries

Combine simple syrup and raspberries in a large
saucepan and cook at medium heat for 20 minutes.
Continue stirring—raspberries should break up into
small pieces and turn a deep pink color. Remove from
heat and, using a chinois strainer or cheesecloth, strain
into a container. Allow to cool to room temperature
before refrigerating. For longer shelf life always keep
refrigerated.

Turn On The Light

TURN ON
THE LIGHT

Style: Shaken

Base: Rum

Ingredients:
1½ ounces Rhum J.M white rum
4 dashes Angostura bitters
4 dashes Peychaud's bitters
½ ounce fresh lime juice
½ ounce simple syrup
1 small bunch loose mint
Topped with club soda

Glass: Pilsner

Ice: Cubed for shaking, crushed for serving

Garnish: Fresh mint tops, bitters float

Tools: Muddler, ounce jigger, Boston shaker,
Hawthorne strainer, fine strainer, mixing spoon

Methodology:
Add mint to serving glass and give it a light muddle,
then set aside. Combine Rhum J.M, lime juice, and
simple syrup in Boston shaker with ice. Shake hard
and double strain into glass with mint. Add crushed
ice, top with club soda, stir, add more ice, then float
bitters at top. Garnish and serve.

Special Ingredients:
Simple Syrup
1½ cups room-temperature water
1½ cups granulated sugar

Combine equal parts water to sugar in a pan over
low heat. Stir until sugar and water have fully
integrated, add orange bitters and stir. Let cool to
room temperature, then refrigerate for 2 hours before
using. For longer shelf life, always keep refrigerated.

Outta My System

OUTTA
MY SYSTEM

Style: Stirred

Base: Cognac

Ingredients:
2 ounces Martell Cognac
1 ounce sweet vermouth
1 teaspoon Suze liqueur
4 dashes Vieux Pontarlier Verte Absinthe
4 dashes Peychaud's bitters

Glass: Coupe

Ice: Cubed for stirring only

Garnish: Orange twist, aged cocktail cherry

Tools: Ounce jigger, mixing glass, mixing spoon,
julep strainer, paring knife or peeler

Methodology:
Combine all ingredients in mixing glass, add as much
ice as possible, and stir for 30 seconds. Strain into
chilled serving glass. Carefully twist the citrus peel
over glass to express oils, and discard peel. Garnish
with cherry, and serve.

Mix'd Girl

MIX'D GIRL

Style: Shaken

Base: Vodka

Ingredients:
1 ounce Ketel One vodka
1 ounce Mr. Black coffee liqueur
¼ ounce amaretto
¼ ounce fresh pineapple juice
¼ ounce fresh lemon juice

Glass: Coupe

Ice: Cubed for shaking only

Garnish: Lemon twist

Tools: Ounce jigger, Boston shaker, Hawthorne strainer, fine strainer, paring knife or peeler

Methodology:
Combine all ingredients in Boston shaker. Dry shake for 10 seconds, then add cubed ice, shake hard, and double strain. Carefully twist the citrus peel over glass to express oils, discard peel, and serve.

Monster Mash

MONSTER MASH

Style: Shaken

Base: Vodka

Ingredients:
1½ ounces Grey Goose Vodka
1½ ounces coconut milk
½ ounce blue curaçao
½ ounce fresh lemon juice
¼ ounce vanilla syrup
1 heaping spoon of honey tapioca balls
2 orange slices

Glass: Highball

Ice: Cubed

Garnish: Shaved macadamia nut, wide straw

Tools: Muddler, ounce jigger, Boston shaker, Hawthorne strainer, fine strainer, microplane, mixing spoon

Methodology:
Add tapioca balls to the bottom of serving glass and set aside. Muddle orange slices in Boston shaker, then add vodka, coconut milk, lemon juice, curaçao, and vanilla syrup. Add ice, shake hard, double strain. Now add ice over the tapioca, doubles train and garnish.

Special Ingredients:
Vanilla Syrup
1 quart 1:1 simple syrup
¼ ounce Madagascar vanilla extract

Combine equal parts water to sugar over low heat. Stir until sugar and water have fully integrated, add vanilla extract and stir. Bring to room temperature then refrigerate for two hours.

FIVE THINGS YOU CAN ALWAYS BLAME ON THE ALCOHOL

1. Memory loss

2. Your actions

3. Agreeing to the wrong business deals

4. Being late to stuff

5. Whiskey dick

Naked On The Dance Floor

NAKED ON THE DANCE FLOOR

Style: Shaken

Base: Vodka

Ingredients:
1½ ounces Sweet Tea–Infused Vodka
½ ounce Limoncello liqueur
½ ounce triple sec
½ ounce fresh lemon juice
½ ounce honey syrup
Topped with Miller High Life beer

Glass: Highball

Ice: Cubed

Garnish: Lemon wheel, fresh mint

Tools: Ounce jigger, Boston shaker, Hawthorne strainer, fine strainer, mixing spoon, paring knife

Methodology:
Combine all ingredients except the beer in Boston shaker. Add ice, give it a hard shake, and double strain into glass. Add ice, top with the High Life, stir, garnish, and serve.

Special Ingredients:
Sweet Tea–Infused Vodka
750 milliliters vodka
½ cup sugar
½ cup water
2 black tea cold-brew tea bags

Combine water and sugar in a bowl and whisk until sugar is dissolved. Add vodka, stir well, and then add tea bags. Store in a quart container with a lid at room temperature for 60 minutes, stirring every 15 minutes.

Remove tea bags when time is up.

Honey Syrup
1 cup premium honey
1 cup water

Combine equal parts water to honey in a pan over low heat. Stir until honey and water have fully integrated. Let cool to room temperature, then refrigerate for 2 hours before use. Shake, stir or agitate at all times of use. Keep for longer shelf, life always keep refrigerated.

Can't Believe It

CAN'T
BELIEVE IT

Style: Built in Glass

Base: Sherry

Ingredients:
2 ounces Manzanilla sherry
½ ounce fresh lemon juice
4 drops CBD oil
Topped with grape soda

Glass: Highball

Ice: Cubed

Garnish: Skewered blueberries, lemon wheel

Tools: Ounce jigger, mixing spoon, paring knife

Methodology:
Build all ingredients in glass, adding grape soda last.
Carefully add ice and top up if needed. Stir, garnish,
and serve.

Neon Lights

NEON LIGHTS

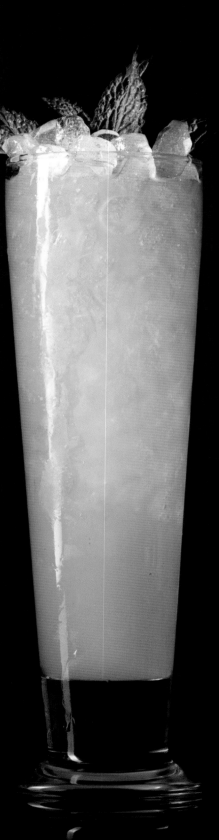

Style: Built in glass and swizzled

Base: Hypnotiq

Ingredients:
2 ounces Hypnotiq
1½ ounces Rockey's liqueur
1 ounce Wray & Nephew rum
1 ounce fresh pineapple juice

Glass: Pilsner

Ice: Crushed

Garnish: Fresh mint

Tools: Ounce jigger, swizzle stick

Methodology:
Build all ingredients in glass. Fill with crushed ice
and swizzle. Top up with more crushed ice, garnish,
and serve.

Nightmare

NIGHTMARE

Style: Shaken

Base: Vodka

Ingredients:
2 ounces Absolut Mandrin vodka
½ ounce triple sec
½ ounce fresh orange juice
4 dashes orange bitters
4 drops orange-flower water
1 pinch sea salt
Topped with orange Coke

Glass: Highball

Ice: Cubed

Garnish: Dehydrated orange wheel, straw

Tools: Ounce jigger, Boston shaker, Hawthorne strainer, fine strainer, mixing spoon

Methodology:
Combine all ingredients except the orange Coke in Boston shaker. Add ice, shake, and double strain into glass. Top with orange Coke, carefully add ice, and top up with more Coke if needed. Stir, garnish, and serve.

Special Ingredients:
Dehydrated Orange Wheel
Dehydrated fruit can be store bought or special ordered.

RED CUP
THINSULATION

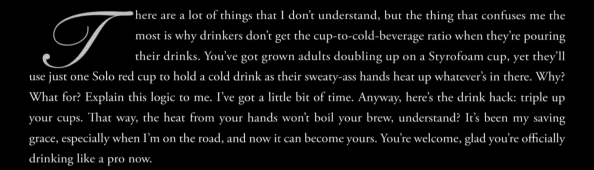

There are a lot of things that I don't understand, but the thing that confuses me the most is why drinkers don't get the cup-to-cold-beverage ratio when they're pouring their drinks. You've got grown adults doubling up on a Styrofoam cup, yet they'll use just one Solo red cup to hold a cold drink as their sweaty-ass hands heat up whatever's in there. Why? What for? Explain this logic to me. I've got a little bit of time. Anyway, here's the drink hack: triple up your cups. That way, the heat from your hands won't boil your brew, understand? It's been my saving grace, especially when I'm on the road, and now it can become yours. You're welcome, glad you're officially drinking like a pro now.

Red Cup

RED CUP

Style: Built in glass

Base: Vodka

Ingredients:
1 ounce Stoli Blueberi vodka
½ ounce crème de cassis
½ ounce fresh lemon juice
3 scoops blackberry sorbet
Topped with White Claw Blackberry hard seltzer

Glass: Solo red cup

Ice: Cubed for shaking, crushed for serving

Garnish: Blueberries, blackberries, shaved lemon
zest, half orange wheel, straw

Tools: Ice cream scoop, ounce jigger, Boston shaker,
Hawthorne strainer, fine strainer, mixing spoon,
paring knife, microplane

Methodology:
Drop up to three large scoops of sorbet into cup so
the final scoop is sticking out the top, then set aside.
Combine vodka, lemon juice, and crème de cassis in
Boston shaker, add ice, and quickly shake. Double
strain over sorbet, then surround sides of sorbet with
crushed ice. Top with White Claw, stir, then add
more shaved ice but do not cover sorbet. Garnish
and serve.

Reggae
Night

REGGAE
NIGHT

Style: Shaken

Base: Cachaça/Rum

Ingredients:
1 ounce Avuá Prata cachaça
1 ounce Avuá Amburana cachaça
1 ounce Appleton Estate rum
½ ounce Pierre Ferrand curaçao
¾ ounce fresh lime juice
¾ ounce orgeat
¼ ounce simple syrup

Glass: Pilsner

Ice: Crushed

Garnish: Shaved nutmeg

Tools: Ounce jigger, Boston shaker, swizzle stick, paring knife

Methodology:
Combine all ingredients in Boston shaker and dry shake for 10 seconds. Pour into glass, fill with crushed ice, and swizzle. Add more crushed ice to top up the glass, garnish, and serve.

Special Ingredients:
Orgeat
Orgeat can be store bought. I recommend BG Reynolds.

Simple Syrup
1½ cups room-temperature water
1½ cups granulated sugar

Combine equal parts water to sugar in a pan over low heat. Stir until sugar and water have fully integrated, add orange bitters and stir. Let cool to room temperature, then refrigerate for 2 hours before using. For longer shelf life, always keep refrigerated.

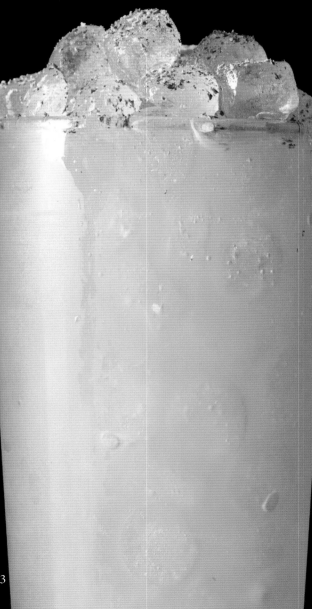

Shawty Get Loose

SHAWTY
GET LOOSE

Style: Stirred

Base: Whiskey

Ingredients:
1 ounce Gentleman Jack whiskey
1 ounce Cinzano sweet vermouth
1 ounce Campari liqueur
½ ounce white crème de cacao

Glass: Coupe

Ice: Cubed for stirring only

Garnish: Aged cocktail cherry

Tools: Ounce jigger, mixing glass, mixing spoon, julep strainer

Methodology:
Combine all ingredients in mixing glass, add as much ice as possible, and stir for 30 seconds. Strain into chilled serving glass, garnish, and serve.

Low

LOW

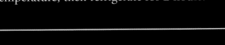

Style: Shaken

Base: Tequila

Ingredients:
1½ ounces Hiatus Tequila Blanco
½ ounce peach liqueur
½ ounce fresh lemon juice
½ ounce grenadine
2 dashes orange bitters

Glass: Coupe

Ice: Cubed for shaking only

Garnish: No garnish

Tools: Ounce jigger, Boston shaker, Hawthorne strainer, fine strainer

Methodology:
Combine all ingredients in Boston shaker, add ice, shake hard, double strain, garnish, and serve.

Special Ingredients:
Grenadine
2 cups pomegranate juice
2 cups Sugar in The Raw
12 dashes orange bitters

Combine the pomegranate juice and sugar in a pan over low heat. Stir until sugar has fully dissolved, add orange bitters, and stir some more. Let cool to room temperature, then refrigerate for 2 hours.

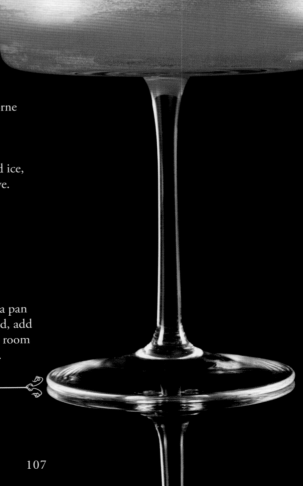

She's A Vibe

SHE'S A VIBE

Style: Stirred

Base: Gin

Ingredients:
½ ounce Bulldog gin
½ ounce Aperol liqueur
½ ounce triple sec
2 dashes orange bitters
2 dashes Angostura bitters
Topped with champagne and club soda

Glass: Wine glass

Ice: Cubed for stirring only

Garnish: Half orange wheel

Tools: Ounce jigger, mixing glass, mixing spoon, julep strainer, paring knife

Methodology:
Combine gin, Aperol, triple sec, and ice in mixing glass add ice and stir for 20 seconds. Pour into serving glass, top with equal parts champagne and club soda, stir, garnish,and serve.

THE LEGEND OF
MY LIQUOR CHAIN(S)

*Y*ears back, you might have seen me rocking a whole diamond-encrusted top shelf around my neck. So I had this idea where I was going to make chains out of every Black-owned liquor brand. Little did I know, most of the brands I made chains out of were only Black people–endorsed and not exactly Black-owned, but whatever. My heart was in the right place. So I would wear all of these chains at the same time—I got up to like ten at once. The goal was that if I crossed paths with one of the owners, then I would hand them off a chain as a gift.

That didn't exactly go as planned. One night I was out and saw Puff, and I tried to give him his Cîroc chain. He would not accept that shit. He thought I was drunk off my ass and randomly trying to be the Good Samaritan of chains and just handing them out, only to regret the whole transaction the next morning. But that was my plan the whole time. He refused, and my whole plan was ruined. Oh well. I have no idea where the hell those chains are anymore, but I hope they're doing well.

What You Want

WHAT YOU WANT

Style: Shaken

Base: Moonshine

Ingredients:
2 ounces Saint Luna moonshine
2 ounces Rockey's liqueur
2 ounces fresh orange juice
1 ounce coconut milk
½ ounce simple syrup
1 drop Madagascar vanilla extract

Glass: Highball

Ice: Cubed for shaking only

Garnish: Shaved lime zest

Tools: Ounce jigger, Boston shaker, Hawthorne strainer, fine strainer, microplane

Methodology:
Combine all ingredients in Boston shaker and dry shake for 15 seconds. Add ice and shake hard for 20 seconds. Double strain into glass, garnish, and serve.

Special Ingredients:
Simple Syrup
1½ cups room-temperature water
1½ cups granulated sugar

Combine equal parts water to sugar in a pan over low heat. Stir until sugar has dissolved, add orange bitters and stir. Let cool to room temperature, then refrigerate for 2 hours before using. For longer shelf life, always keep refrigerated.

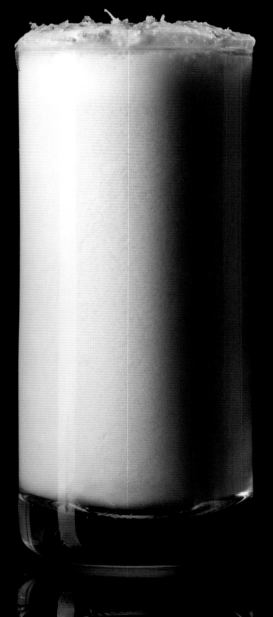

Soul On Fire

SOUL
ON FIRE

Style: Built in glass and swizzled

Base: Cognac

Ingredients:
2 ounces Hennessy Cognac
½ ounce Velvet Falernum liqueur
¾ ounce fresh grapefruit juice
¾ ounce cinnamon syrup
6 dashes Angostura Lime Cup filled with 151 Rum

Glass: Hurricane glass

Ice: Crushed

Garnish: Flaming Lime Cup

Tools: Ounce jigger, swizzle stick, microplane

Methodology:
Build all ingredients in glass. Fill with crushed ice and
swizzle. Add more crushed ice to top up the glass,
garnish, and serve.

Special Ingredients:
Cinnamon Syrup
1 quart 1:1 simple syrup
6 sticks cinnamon

In a container with a lid, add cinnamon to simple
syrup at room temperature. Cover with lid and allow
to macerate in the refrigerator for 48 hours. Routinely
agitate the container by giving it a good shake. Before
using a strainer or colander, remove cinnamon from
container and re-bottle the syrup for later use.

Flaming Lime Cup
1 half of fresh lime
1 sugar cube
¼ ounce 151-proof rum

Soak sugar cube in 151 rum and set aside. Using a
citrus reamer, squeeze juice and pulp out of half a lime
until the inside is in the shape of a shallow cup. Drop
the cube into the lime cup. When the drink is ready to
serve, set fire to the sugar cube and place the lime cup
in drink.

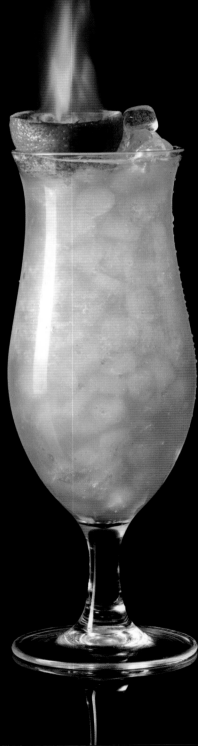

Suicide

SUICIDE

Style: Shaken

Base: Tequila

Ingredients:
1½ ounces Ghost-Pepper Espolon Tequila Blanco
¾ ounce dry vermouth
1 ounce fresh pineapple juice
¼ ounce fresh lime juice

Glass: Double rocks

Ice: Cubed for shaking only

Garnish: Aged cocktail cherry, dehydrated pineapple

Tools: Ounce jigger, Boston shaker, Hawthorne strainer, fine strainer

Methodology:
Combine all ingredients in Boston shaker, add ice, shake hard, double strain into glass, garnish, and serve.

Special Ingredients:
Ghost-Pepper-Espolon Tequila Blanco
750 milliliters bottle of Espolon Tequila Blanco
1 sliced ghost pepper

Combine all ingredients in a quart container with a lid. Give it a nice shake and let sit for 30 minutes. Routinely taste to determine level of heat. It should have a good kick but not so strong that you can't knock it back. Peppers vary in heat scale, so you will need to keep checking. Double infusion time if it does not pick up enough heat.

Dehydrated Pineapple
Dehydrated fruit can be store bought or special ordered.

I'M N LUV
(WIT A STRIPPER)

Style: Shaken

Base: Brandy

Ingredients:
2 ounces Hennessy Cognac
½ ounce crème de cacao
½ ounce crème de fraise
1 ounce heavy cream

Glass: Snifter

Ice: Large cube for serving, cubed for shaking

Garnish: Shaved dark chocolate

Tools: Ounce jigger, Boston shaker, Hawthorne strainer, fine strainer, microplane

Methodology:
Combine all ingredients in Boston Shaker and dry shake for 10 seconds. Add ice, hard shake for 15 seconds, double strain, garnish, and serve.

Sweet

SWEET

Style: Stirred

Base: Bourbon

Ingredients:
2 ounces Fistful of Bourbon
¾ ounce sweet vermouth
½ ounce Cherry Heering

Glass: Coupe

Ice: Cubed for stirring only

Garnish: Orange twist, aged cocktail cherry

Tools: Ounce jigger, mixing glass, mixing spoon, julep strainer, paring knife or peeler

Methodology:
Build all ingredients in mixing glass, add as much ice as possible, and stir for 30 seconds. Strain into chilled serving glass, garnish, and serve.

Textin' My Ex

MY EX

Style: Shaken

Base: Gin/Vodka/Rum

Ingredients:
½ ounce gin
½ ounce vodka
½ ounce rum
½ ounce Pierre Ferrand curaçao
½ ounce fresh lemon juice
½ ounce raspberry syrup
Topped with vanilla Coke

Glass: Highball

Ice: Cubed

Garnish: Orange wheel, skewered raspberries

Tools: Ounce jigger, Boston shaker, Hawthorne strainer, fine strainer, paring knife

Methodology:
Combine all ingredients except the vanilla Coke in Boston shaker. Add ice, give it a hard shake, and double strain into glass. Add ice, top with vanilla Coke, garnish, and serve.

Special Ingredients:
Raspberry Syrup
1 quart 1:1 simple syrup (room temperature)
1 pint raspberries

Combine simple syrup and raspberries in a large saucepan and cook at medium heat for 20 minutes. Continue stirring—raspberries should break up into small pieces and turn a deep pink color. Remove from heat and, using a chinois strainer or cheesecloth, strain into a container. Allow to cool to room temperature before refrigerating.

TIME MACHINE

Style: Built in glass and swizzled

Base: Whiskey

Ingredients:
2 ounces Gentleman Jack whiskey
¼ ounce Suze liqueur
4 dashes celery bitters
½ ounce honey syrup
1 small bunch loose mint
Celery ribbons

Glass: Julep tin

Ice: Crushed

Garnish: Fresh mint, celery ribbon, powdered sugar

Tools: Muddler, ounce jigger, swizzle stick, Y peeler

Methodology:
Muddle celery ribbons and fresh mint in julep tin, then discard from tin. Build the rest of the ingredients in the julep tin. Add crushed ice, swizzle for 10 seconds, and add more crushed ice until it is packed to the very top. Garnish and serve.

Special Ingredient:
Honey Syrup
1 cup premium honey
1 cup water

Combine equal parts water to honey in a pan over low heat. Stir until honey and water have fully integrated. Let cool to room temperature, then refrigerate for 2 hours before use. Shake, stir or agitate at all times of use. For longer shelf, life always keep refrigerated.

Blame It

BLAME IT

Style: Shaken

Base: Tequila

Ingredients:
1 ounce Hiatus Tequila Blanco
½ ounce Grapefruit Cordial
½ ounce fresh lime juice
6 drops saline solution
Topped with White Claw grapefruit hard seltzer

Glass: Collins

Ice: Cubed

Garnish: Grapefruit spear, fresh mint

Tools: Ounce jigger, Boston shaker, Hawthorne strainer, fine strainer, mixing spoon, paring knife

Methodology:
Combine all ingredients except the White Claw in Boston shaker. Add ice and give a hard shake, then double strain into glass over ice. Top with White Claw and stir. Top up again if needed, garnish, and serve.

Special Ingredients:
Grapefruit Sherbet/Cordial
1½ cups fresh white grapefruit juice
1½ cups granulated sugar
Peels from 4 grapefruits

Place grapefruit juice and sugar in a blender and blend on high until all the sugar has dissolved. Pour contents into a quart container. Twist all grapefruit peels into the grapefruit-and-sugar mix to get as much grapefruit oil as possible. Add peels to the container and secure lid. Give it a nice 15-second shake, then refrigerate for a minimum of 12 hours, grapefruit skins can be removed and strained after this period of time.

Saline Solution
1 cup kosher salt
1 cup water

Combine water and salt over low heat. Stir until salt has fully dissolved. Let cool to room temperature, then refrigerate for 2 hours before use. Fill a dropper bottle to use in small quantities; store the remainder in a tightly sealed quart container and keep refrigerated.

Up Down

UP DOWN

Style: Shaken

Base: Cognac

Ingredients:
2 ounces Martell Cognac
1 ounce Kahúla coffee liqueur
2 dashes green cardamom bitters
2 ounces coconut milk

Glass: Snifter

Ice: Large cube for serving, cubed for shaking

Garnish: Shaved pistachio

Tools: Ounce jigger, Boston shaker, Hawthorne strainer, fine strainer, mixing spoon, microplane

Methodology:
Combine all ingredients in Boston shaker. Dry shake for 15 seconds, then add ice, shake for 15 seconds, double strain, add ice cube, garnish, and serve.

Special Ingredient:
Green Cardamom Bitters
Green cardamom bitters can be store bought or special ordered. I recommend Scrappy's.

WAKE UP DEAD

Style: Stirred

Base: Jägermeister/Rum

Ingredients:
½ ounce Jägermeister
1 ounce Diplomático Reserva Exclusiva rum
1 ounce Mr. Black coffee liqueur
¼ ounce cinnamon syrup

Glass: Double rocks

Ice: Large cube for serving, cubed for stirring

Garnish: Lemon twist, lemon spiral, aged cocktail cherry

Tools: Ounce jigger, mixing glass, mixing spoon, julep strainer, paring knife or peeler, channel knife

Methodology:
Prepare a frozen serving glass. Combine all ingredients in mixing glass. Add cubed ice, stir for 20 seconds, and strain into serving glass. Carefully twist the citrus peel over glass to express oils, and discard peel. Add the rest of the garnishes, and serve.

Special Ingredients:
Cinnamon Syrup
1 quart 1:1 simple syrup
6 sticks cinnamon

In a container with a lid, add cinnamon to simple syrup at room temperature. Cover with lid and allow to macerate in the refrigerator for 48 hours. Routinely agitate container during this time. Using a strainer or colander, remove cinnamon from container and re-bottle the syrup for later use.

MIX-IN CHEAT CODES

 f you're trying to really add some pizzazz to your dranks, you've gotta know what the hell you're doing, which also includes what the hell to buy at the damn store. We broke that down for you, but I'll let my man Maxwell take it from here. BYE! (T-Pain)

Store-Bought Ingredients

Dehydrated Pineapple
Dehydrated Orange Wheels
Candied Orange
Dehydrated and candied fruit can be store bought or special ordered.

Candied Ginger
Candied ginger can be store bought or special ordered.

Blueberry Jam
Blueberry jam or preserves can be store bought. I recommend Bonne Maman Wild Blueberry Preserves.

Celery Bitters
Celery bitters can be store bought. I recommend The Bitter Truth bitters.

Guava Purée
Guava purée can be store bought or special ordered. I recommend The Perfect Purée.

Matcha Powder
Matcha powder can be store bought. I recommend Jade Leaf Culinary Matcha.

Orgeat
Orgeat can be store bought. I recommend BG Reynolds.

Green Cardamom Bitters
Green cardamom bitters can be store bought or special ordered. I recommend Scrappy's.

Prepared Spirits

Jalapeño-Infused Tequila

750 milliliters tequila

3–4 sliced green jalapeños without seeds

Combine all ingredients in a quart container with a lid. Give it a nice shake and let sit for 30 minutes. Routinely taste to determine level of heat. It should have a good kick but not so strong that you can't knock it back. Peppers vary in heat scale, so you will need to keep checking.

Fennel-Infused Gin

6 bulbs of fresh fennel

750 milliliters dry gin

Finely chop fennel bulbs and put in 1-gallon Ziploc plastic bag. Add gin, seal tightly, and refrigerate with bag sitting upright for 24 hours. Strain out fennel and re-bottle gin for use.

Olde English Reduction

5 cups Olde English malt liquor

4 cinnamon sticks

4 anise pods

6 cardamom pods

5 cups granulated sugar

In a large saucepan, add Olde English and spices. Heat to a simmer on medium, 10 minutes. Once liquid is indicated as heated, reduce heat to low and slowly stir in sugar. Once all sugar has been fully dissolved, bring heat back up to a simmer. Periodically stir for 30 minutes. Remove from heat and allow to cool to room temperature. Let chill in the fridge in a uncovered nonmetal container. Strain out spices before using in recipe and keep refrigerated covered for long term shelf life.

Sweet Tea–Infused Vodka

750 milliliters vodka

½ cup sugar

½ cup water

2 black tea cold-brew tea bags

Combine water and sugar in a bowl and whisk until sugar is dissolved. Add vodka, stir well, and then add tea bags. Store in a quart container with a lid at room temperature for 60 minutes, stirring every 15 minutes. Remove tea bags when time is up.

Ghost Pepper Rye Whiskey

750 milliliters whiskey

1 sliced ghost pepper

Combine all ingredients in a quart container with a lid. Give it a nice shake and let sit for 30 minutes. Routinely taste to determine level of heat. It should have a good kick but not so strong that you can't knock it back. Peppers vary in heat scale, so you will need to keep checking. Double infusion time if it does not pick up enough heat.

Garnishes

Smoked Chipotle Salt Rimmer

1 tablespoon smoked salt

1 tablespoon smoked paprika

½ tablespoon Tajín seasoning

Combine all ingredients in a mortar and grind up with pestle for uniform coarse texture.

Flaming Lime Cup

1 half lime

1 sugar cube

¼ ounce 151-proof rum

Soak sugar cube in 151 rum and set aside. Using a citrus reamer, squeeze juice and pulp out of half a lime until the inside is in the shape of a shallow cup. Drop the cube into the lime cup. When the drink is ready to serve, set fire to the sugar cube and place the lime cup in drink.

Syrups and Solutions

Simple Syrup

Room-temperature water

Granulated sugar

Combine equal parts water to sugar in a pan over low heat. Stir until sugar has dissolved. Let cool to room temperature, then refrigerate for 2 hours before using. For longer shelf life, always keep refrigerated.

Syrups and Solutions cont.

Honey Syrup
Premium honey
Water

Combine equal parts water to honey in a pan over low heat. Stir until honey and water have fully integrated. Let cool to room temperature, then refrigerate for 2 hours before use. For longer shelf, life always keep refrigerated.

Spicy Honey Syrup
1 cup premium honey
1 cup water
1 small sliced jalapeño

Combine water and honey in a pan over low heat. Stir until honey and water have fully integrated. Add sliced jalapeño and simmer for 15 minutes. Let cool to room temperature, then refrigerate for 1 hour. Strain to remove jalapeño. For longer shelf, life always keep refrigerated.

Coconut Syrup
Coconut milk
Coconut cream

Combine equal parts coconut milk to coconut cream in a pan over low heat for 15 minutes. Let cool to room temperature, then refrigerate for 2 hours. For longer shelf life, always refrigerate. Be sure to give the syrup a shake or stir before using.

Raspberry Syrup
1 quart simple syrup
1 pint raspberries

Combine simple syrup and raspberries in a large saucepan and cook at medium heat for 20 minutes. Continue stirring—raspberries should break up into small pieces and turn a deep pink color. Remove from heat and, using a chinois strainer or cheese cloth, strain into a container. Allow to cool to room temperature before refrigerating.

Syrups and Solutions cont.

Vanilla Syrup
1 quart 1:1 simple syrup
¼ ounce Madagascar vanilla extract

Combine vanilla extra to pre-made simple syrup, using a whisk or spoon, whisk extract until completely dissolved.

Grenadine
2 cups pomegranate juice
2 cups Sugar in The Raw
12 dashes orange bitters

Combine the pomegranate juice and sugar in a pan over low heat. Stir until sugar has fully dissolved, add orange bitters, and stir some more. Let cool to room temperature, then refrigerate for 2 hours.

Cinnamon Syrup
1 quart simple syrup
6 sticks cinnamon

In a container with a lid, add cinnamon to simple syrup at room temperature. Cover with lid and allow to macerate in the refrigerator for 48 hours. Agitate the container by giving the container a good shake before using a strainer or colander, remove cinnamon from container and re-bottle the syrup for later use.

Grapefruit Cordial
1½ cups fresh white grapefruit juice
1½ cups granulated sugar
Peels from 4 grapefruits

Place grapefruit juice and sugar in a blender and blend on high until all the sugar has dissolved. Pour contents into a quart container. Twist all grapefruit peels into the grapefruit-and-sugar mix to get as much grapefruit oil as possible. Add peels to the container and secure lid. Give it a nice 15-second shake, then refrigerate for a minimum of 12 hours, grapefruit skins can be removed and strained after this period of time.

Syrups and Solutions cont.

Saline Solution

1 cup kosher salt

1 cup water

Combine water and salt over low heat. Stir until salt has fully dissolved. Let cool to room temperature, then refrigerate for 2 hours before use. Fill a dropper bottle to use in small quantities; store the remainder in a tightly sealed quart container and keep refrigerated.

ACKNOWLEDGMENTS

first wanna thank everybody who has had to deal with drunk T-Pain. I mean, everybody: friends, family, doctors, nurses, complete strangers at that bar in Wyoming. Everybody.

It's kinda like we all have a book now, right?! Ok, no but, ya know?! I most of all wanna thank the person who's had to deal with this shit more than anyone, MY WIFE *Borat voice*.

I can already tell you, that in order for me to come up with 50 drinks was a feat, BUT, for her to stand by and watch me try them all and still put up with me is just super human. Thank you, you magnificent woman.

I wanna thank Kathy Iandoli for dealing with my drunk Zoom calls and translating my drunk talk into actual words and making a dope ass book out of it. Couldn't have done it without you. Thank you.

I guess at some point I should thank all my enablers. Thanx. You're all assholes.

Bye. Read the book. Don't just put it on a table or some shit.

Love,
Your local jester
T-Pain

Kingston Imperial

Marvis Johnson – Publisher

Kathy Iandoli – Editorial Director

Joshua Wirth – Designer

Kristin Clifford – Publicist, Finn Partners

Emilie Moran – Publicist, Finn Partners

Contact:

Kingston Imperial

144 North 7th Street #255

Brooklyn, NY 11249

Email: Info@kingstonimperial.com

www.kingstonimperial.com

Copyright ©2021 by Faheem Rasheed Najm

Photography copyright ©2021 by Madelynne Ross of Bites and Bevs LLC. and Kingston Imperial, LLC.
Styling by Proper Garnish LLC.

Kingston Imperial is committed to publishing works of quality and integrity. In that spirit, we are proud to offer th book to our readers; however, the story, the experiences, and the words are the author's alone.

All Rights Reserved.

For information address Kingston Imperial, LLC
Rights Department, 144 North 7th Street, #255 Brooklyn N.Y. 11249

Published by Kingston Imperial, LLC
www.kingstonimperial.com

Cataloging in Publication data is on file with the library of Congress

Can I Mix You A Drink? T-Pain with Maxwell Britten. Curated by Kathy Iandoli.
Photographs by Madelynne Ross of Bites and Bevs LLC

Hardcover ISBN:9781954220003
Ebook ISBN: 9781954220010

Printed in China

Design by Joshua Wirth of PixiLL Designs, LLC

First Edition

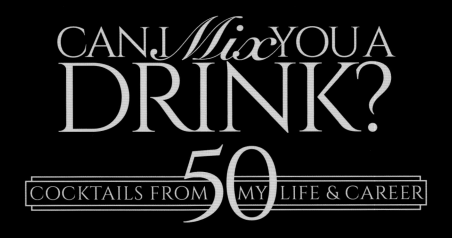

CAN I *Mix* YOU A DRINK?

50 COCKTAILS FROM MY LIFE & CAREER

T-PAIN

with MAXWELL BRITTEN